MW00417108

Walking Durango

HISTORY, SIGHTS,
and STORIES

Peggy Winkworth

Published in collaboration with the La Plata County Historical Society

Peggy Winkworth

ISBN: 978-1-887805-37-7
Library of Congress Control Number: 2013942096

Editor: Elizabeth A. Green
Design and Layout: Lisa Snider Atchison

www.thedurangoheraldsmallpress.com

Get Ready,

Kids, adults, visitors, locals—anyone might be curious about downtown Durango. It is a fascinating, historical town. This book is designed to help you explore the town and learn a bit about some of its early buildings and residents.

As you walk along the route outlined on the back cover, try to find the items in the photographs. Think of the tour as a sort of scavenger hunt. If you don't see the item in the picture, you will find a clue to its location on the next page, along with related facts and stories to enlighten, amuse, and inform you about the sights you are seeing and the people who built Durango.

The tour will take you through two National Historic Districts and past several individual National Historic Landmarks. The landmarks and the buildings and homes that contribute to the Historic District designations will be identified.

All the sites pictured are on or within walking distance of Main Avenue. The route begins at the Durango & Silverton Railroad Depot at the south end of town and continues north to 12th Street, then moves east to 3rd Avenue and proceeds south again to College Drive with a short detour to 2nd Avenue, then back to Main – a full "circle."

FYI:
You'll be on public property throughout this tour, so take all the photos you want. Please don't go on private property, for any reason, without the owner's permission.

The complete tour is about 1½ miles long and can be completed in 1½ to 2 hours. It can easily be divided into segments to accommodate time restrictions or interests.

Have fun! Take your camera!

Take a water bottle – it's Durangoans' favorite accessory.
Use crosswalks – you have the right-of-way.
We're at high altitude – take your time and rest along the way.
Stop for refreshments at one of our many restaurants.

KEY:

 You found it!

Registered National Historic Landmark

Contributor to Historic District: when it was established:
Main Avenue, 1980; East Third Avenue, 1984

★ City of Durango Historic Landmark

Bold face type in the text will identify individuals in photographs.

Get Set,

People have lived along the Animas River for thousands of years. Wildlife and water met the needs of Paleo Indians, followed by Ancestral Puebloans, and, eventually, Utes. In the early 1860s, the discovery of gold and silver in the mountains of Southwest Colorado brought fortune-seeking prospectors and miners. Farmers and families followed, lured by free land for homesteaders. After the American Civil War came the railroads. Durango was incorporated as a town in 1881, and was linked with the Silverton mining district by rail in 1882.

Abundant coal fueled smelters and water irrigated farmland. While other western towns sprang up and disappeared almost overnight, Durango endured. Though it was rough around the edges in the early days, Durango's founders envisioned the town as proper and civilized. The Denver & Rio Grande Railroad's real estate company mapped it out: Main Avenue and 2nd Avenue for businesses, and 3rd Avenue for a wide residential boulevard with trees down the middle. Eighty lots were sold as soon as they went on sale in September 1880.

In 1889, fire roared through the town, destroying numerous businesses, churches, and homes. Residents rebuilt, many with more fire-resistant materials. Fire has continued to play a role in shaping the look of the town.

America's economic swings have impacted Durango, but growth has continued, fueled in part by the discovery of large deposits of oil and gas in the 1950s. Fort Lewis College moved into town and expanded from a two-year agricultural school to a four-year college. Scenic attractions and outdoor diversions encouraged tourism, along with proximity to Mesa Verde National Park, the opening of Purgatory Ski Area (now Durango Mountain Resort) in 1965, and transformation of the Durango & Silverton Narrow Gauge Railroad line into a tourist attraction.

Buildings help tell our history, reflecting our origins and changing times. Preserving that history is important to us, so the city of Durango encourages business owners to honor their buildings' original architecture.

With this book in hand, enjoy some of the facts about the town and stories of the people and events that have made Durango what you see today.

(If you're interested in learning more about Durango's past, see the resource listings at the back of the book.)

... Go!

Standing at the southernmost end of Main Avenue,
look for the clue pictured here.

 You have found a lantern on the train station.

THE D&SNGRR

The Durango & Silverton Narrow Gauge Railroad was originally the Denver & Rio Grande Railway. It was built in the early 1880s to transport gold and silver ore from the mines around Silverton to Durango and to transport coal and supplies in the opposite direction. It was an extension of a line that connected Durango to Antonito, Colorado, approximately 150 miles to the east. Part of this line operates today as the Cumbres & Toltec Scenic Railroad between Antonito and Chama, New Mexico.

The **Durango depot** was built in 1881-82, making it one of the town's oldest buildings.

NARROW GAUGE

The term "narrow gauge" refers to the width of the tracks. The rails of narrow gauge tracks are only three feet apart while standard gauge tracks measure 4' 8" in width. (Not coincidentally, this was the distance between the wheels of a Roman chariot.) The narrower tracks were easier to construct through the tight curves and steep mountains of Southwest Colorado, and they were more economical, using less material and requiring smaller cars and engines. There are 45.2 miles of narrow gauge track between Durango and Silverton. Steam locomotives pull most of the trains.

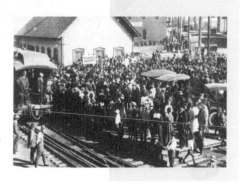

TRAIN MOVIES

A number of Hollywood movies have been shot in Durango featuring the Durango & Silverton Railroad and depot. *A Ticket to Tomahawk,* filmed in 1950 by 20th Century Fox, was a musical comedy about a competitive race between the train and a stagecoach. A young actress named Marilyn Monroe had a small role as a chorus girl in the movie. A replica of the **Emma Sweeny**, the engine that played a role in that film, can be seen in Santa Rita Park on South Camino del Rio.

Another movie, *Around the World in Eighty Days,* a 1956 United Artists film starring David Niven and Shirley MacLaine, had actor Cantinflas crawling along the top of the moving train to reach the engine in an effort to replace the engineer who had been killed by attacking Indians. Needless to say, the passengers were saved.

Butch Cassidy and the Sundance Kid with Paul Newman and Robert Redford and *Support Your Local Gunfighter* with James Garner and Suzanne Pleshette are other popular movies that featured the Durango & Silverton train.

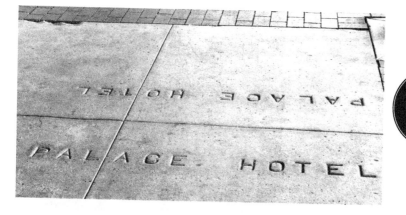

Walk north from the depot; look carefully at the sidewalk.

The name of a historic business is imprinted in the cement where it once stood.

....

THE PALACE

The Palace Hotel no longer exists at this location, though there are still some refurbished rooms of the old hotel in the second story of the building (used

Center of Southwest Studies

by the General Palmer Hotel). The original Palace Hotel ceased operation in the 1930s.

EARLY HOTELS

At various times around the turn of the last century there were three different hotels on this side of the block: the Palace next to the depot, the National in the middle of the block, and the Savoy on the corner. These were among the less expensive hotels in Durango because of noise and soot from the trains in the rail yard.

PAVEMENT

Sidewalks in early Durango were made of wood, and streets were not paved. Flat stones were placed in the muddy streets between boardwalks so pedestrians

could cross without walking through the muck. After citizens began to demand improvements, cement sidewalks gradually replaced the boardwalks along Main Avenue between 1908 and 1915, and the street was paved in 1924.

Walk north along Main Avenue.
From the middle of the block, look at the roofline across the street.

THOMSEN'S STORE

Nels T. Thomsen had this building on the end constructed between 1905 and 1910 to house his secondhand store where he sold such items as miners' supplies, stoves, furniture, and hardware. The date "1913" tells us not when the store was first built but rather the year the second story was added.

N.T. Thomsen building, 1913, now home to a modern-day coffee spot.

ETHNIC BUSINESSES

Over the years, the buildings on this block have housed a variety of businesses including hotels, boarding houses, and saloons. Around the turn of the century, they catered mainly to immigrants who arrived in Durango to work on the railroad or in the nearby mines and smelters. These establishments offered the newcomers comfortable places to live and socialize.

FIORINI BUILDING

Directly across from the parking lot, you'll see the "Fiorini Building," named for John Fiorini. At one time, he lived with his family on the south end of this property in a home that once belonged to his wife's grandmother. The house, of clapboard, stone, and stucco construction, was built in 1881 and was demolished in 1985.

Fiorini operated a men's clothing store until 1930 when the economic decline of the Great Depression forced him out of business. He then ran a monument shop, carving memorial headstones in a studio behind his house. Fiorini learned to carve marble as a young man in Marble, Colorado, where he had worked as a sculptor on the façade for the national Lincoln Memorial.

Continue north to the corner, turn around and look up.

The **General Palmer House clock** is on the corner of the General Palmer Hotel.

THE HOTEL

The structure on this corner was erected in 1898 to house the **Savoy Hotel.** At various times, the building has contained a drug store, a grocery store, and a saloon. The General Palmer Hotel has occupied the site since 1964.

GENERAL PALMER

The hotel is named for **Gen. William Jackson Palmer**, a Medal of Honor recipient who fought in the Union cavalry during the Civil War. After the war, Palmer was a founder of the Denver & Rio Grande Railway Company. The Denver & Rio Grande reached Durango in 1881. Though Palmer never lived here, his railroad played a major role in the design of early Durango, which was laid out much as you see it today.

General Palmer founded Colorado Springs where he lived from 1871 until his death in 1909 at the age of 72.

Cross Main Avenue diagonally (it's legal only at this intersection) and walk north on Main Avenue. At the middle of the block, look across the street for this sign.

 You have found an A. Coors sign, on top of an old **Coors Brewery**.

THE BREWERY

Around the turn of the 20th century, as Durango grew, four different breweries operated in town. One was the Adolph Coors Company, a branch of the original Coors Brewery in Golden, Colorado. Coors built this building in 1900 and continued in business here until the state of Colorado outlawed the manufacture and distribution of alcoholic beverages in 1916, three years before National Prohibition became law in 1919. The brewery was converted to produce soft drinks, the name changed to Durango Bottling Works, and the business sold to a local merchant, John Kellenberger.

JOHN KELLENBERGER

In 1880, a good-natured young man named **John Kellenberger** arrived in the United States from Switzerland. He owned a bakery in Breckenridge, Colorado, and wineries in California before coming to Durango in 1892. He opened a saloon on Main Avenue where he sold liquor, wine, and cigars. He bottled his own Raspberry Julep, a drink renowned throughout the San Juan Basin. Kellenberger was caught illegally smuggling whiskey from Chama, New Mexico, to Telluride, Colorado. He subsequently turned his full attention to the bottling works and opened the first Coca-Cola franchise in Durango.

Look up to find this light fixture.

You are looking at a light fixture on an old Pepsi Cola bottling plant.

THE BUILDING

In the 1920s, this building housed the Handy Auto Sales and Service business. In the 1950s, Pepsi Cola was bottled here.

 Walk ahead to the corner and stop.

THE HANGING

You are now standing where the only **legal hanging** in Durango took place on June 23, 1882. George Woods had been convicted of murdering M.C. Buchanan after an argument at the Pacific Club Saloon. A large crowd turned out to see justice done.

INDIAN ENCAMPMENT

Across 7th Street (the northeast corner of the intersection) was a vacant lot where Southern Ute Indians from south of Durango used to camp from time to time when they came into town to trade or receive government allotments.

Look across Main Avenue and find these pretty corbels.

THE  STRATER HOTEL

In 1886, an enterprising young pharmacist named Henry Strater from Cleveland, Ohio, borrowed money from his father to build a first-class hotel in Durango. Completed in 1888 at a cost of $70,000, the Strater House held fifty guest rooms and the Strater pharmacy. In the office behind the front desk, the hotel's original safe still sits (now empty) with the words "Strater House" and the date, 1888, on the side.

This is the **Strater Hotel**, a Durango landmark for more than 100 years.

HISTORY

From the start the Strater Hotel was a popular, high-quality hotel, but **Henry Strater** and his partner, H.L. Rice, had disagreements about the leasing of the pharmacy. This caused Henry to move his pharmacy north to the corner of 8th Street and Main and, in 1893, to construct the Columbian Hotel directly south of the Strater.

For two years, the Columbian competed with the Strater. Henry's wife, a concert pianist, performed in the Columbian's opera house. However, in an economic downturn, Henry lost both his hotels to the Bank of Cleveland and left for Denver, eventually becoming a tobacco merchant in Cuba. The Columbian merged with the Strater, and the hotel was managed by Durangoans Charles Stilwell, a restaurateur, and Hattie Mashburn, the Strater's head housekeeper. For twenty-four years they kept the business running through good times and bad. It is said that Hattie grew wealthy operating a brothel on the hotel's fourth floor.

THE BARKER FAMILY

Earl Barker Sr. and business partners purchased the declining hotel in 1926. Barker became sole owner in 1954, and the family still owns and runs the Strater.

The Diamond Belle Saloon opened in 1957 bearing the nickname of a Silverton woman who wore a diamond stud in her front tooth. The back bar came originally from Silverton complete with a bullet hole from a shooting there. By 1911, the bar was in **Koshak's Saloon** across from the Durango depot.

The Strater lobby features memorabilia and fine walnut furniture from the Victorian era. Many

famous people have been guests of the hotel, including presidential candidate John Kennedy, past President Gerald Ford, comedian Will Rogers, war hero and actor Audie Murphy, author Louis L'Amour, and movie stars Marilyn Monroe, Paul Newman, and Jimmy Stewart.

☞ **Cross 7th Street and continue north along Main Avenue, looking across the street as you go.**

STUART'S OF DURANGO

Mid-century prosperity brought the sleek, streamlined art moderne look to downtown, seen here in Stuart's of Durango. When Nate Stein took over the store from his father and brother in 1944, he brought this new look with him from New York. He replaced the building's outdated Victorian façade with the curved frontage and unadorned glazed tiles you see and used neon lighting inside and out. Nate Stein's became Stuart's when Stuart Johnson purchased the business in the 1950s. When the sign was changed, the top hat and cane were added.

8

As you near 8th Street, look across Main Avenue for this façade.

You have found the Graden Mercantile Building, founded in 1881. The façade was remodeled in 1985-86.

THOMAS GRADEN

In the 1880s and '90s, **Thomas Graden** operated a drug and paint store, a general store, and a wholesale grocery store in the block where the current Graden Mercantile Company building now stands. He also owned a lumber company and a flour mill, and was a stockholder in the town's "electric railroad" along Main Avenue.

According to local legend and partially corroborated in a 1945 article by Mary Sloan Ayers (daughter of Graden's business partner) copper coins were considered a nuisance in the early days of the mercantile business. Graden had his cashier throw all the pennies from the cash drawer on the floor at the end of each day, to be swept up by the janitor. It is said that children would hurry to collect the pennies before they were swept away, then use them to buy penny candy.

ROBERT E. SLOAN

In 1914, Thomas Graden sold his share in the Mercantile and moved to Hollywood, California. His partner, Robert E. Sloan, took over the business but retained the Graden name. The business has remained in the Sloan family since that time.

FIRE

In February 1948, the Graden Mercantile building was severely damaged by fire and was rebuilt by Robert Sloan's offspring.

Sixty years later, in February 2008, another serious downtown Durango fire occurred approximately where you are standing. A restaurant grease fire spread to destroy three historic buildings (764 to 752 Main Ave.). As you can see, the ruined buildings have been replaced.

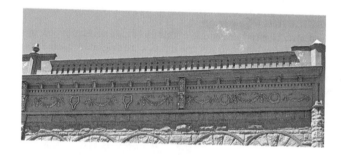

9

Find this ornate border on the corner of 8th and Main.

CHARLES NEWMAN

Charles Newman had the imposing Newman Building erected in 1892. He owned a number of drug stores in Southwest Colorado, including one of the first in Durango. He made a fortune investing in mines near Rico, Colorado, and became an influential businessman and politician.

 You have found the **Newman Block**.

THE BUILDING

The distinctive red sandstone of this building came from nearby quarries. Inside, steam heat and electric lights were originally used throughout, marking the building as very fine and modern in its day. There was even an elevator inside—the only one for hundreds of miles around. In 2009, a fire in the Newman Building was brought under control before the building was destroyed.

TENANTS

Durango's biggest banking crisis hit in December 1907 when the first tenant of this building, Smelter National Bank, shut its doors for good. Three days earlier, Colorado State Bank, a block north on Main Avenue, also had failed. Newspaper owner David Day called the banks "robbers of women and children" because of their poor financial practices. Only the more conservative First National Bank of Durango survived. From the late 1930s to the 1980s, 20th Century Fox owned the **Kiva movie theater**, located at the back of the Newman Building.

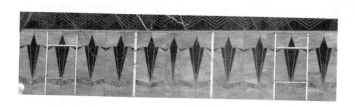

Crossing to the west side of Main Avenue, continue north from the Newman Building. Looking east now, across the street, try to locate these.

 This is one of the first brick buildings in downtown Durango.

CARRARA GLASS

This brick structure was built in the 1880s. Over the years the façades of these stores have been updated and changed.

Of particular interest are the blue, black, and green designs surrounded by black marble over the store on the left. Popular in the Art Deco period of the 1930s and early '40s, these decorative Carrara tiles are now rare. Carrara glass tiles are no longer manufactured. Broken panes in this pattern could not have been replaced and repaired to their present appearance had it not been for the discovery of a stash of Carrara glass in a local man's storage shed where it had been since the 1940s.

MAIN MALL

Behind you, where the Main Mall now stands, an arson fire destroyed six historic buildings in August 1974. The fire started before dawn on a Saturday morning. A fireman and a policeman died in an explosion caused by the blaze. The arsonist was captured, convicted, and sent to prison.

Cross 9th Street, then look back to find this.

 You are looking at details that grace the corner of the **Gardenswartz Building**.

THE BUILDING

This handsome Italian Renaissance style brick building was constructed in 1883 by the Durango Land & Trust Co, the real estate branch of the Denver & Rio Grande Railroad, to stimulate sales and encourage the use of brick and stone. The corner is chamfered (cut off) with an ornamented pediment at the top. It was originally named for Isaac Kruschke who operated a dry goods store here. Purchased by Lester Gardenswartz in the 1920s and owned by his family for decades, it is now called the Gardenswartz Building.

FIRE

In December 1907, just two weeks before two nearby banks failed, the building on the southeast corner of this intersection burned and was soon replaced by the current structure. Before the fire and after, the corner space was occupied by Parsons Drug Store, a favorite spot among Durangoans for its soda fountain until the business closed in 1992.

Look for this sign on the building beside you.

THE BANK

In 1881, a dynamic young banker named **Alfred Phineas (A.P.) Camp** moved the Bank of the San Juan south from nearby Animas City to Durango. When the bank moved into its new home, it was renamed the Bank of Durango. Its only competitor was First National Bank, chartered in 1882.

 You have found the original location of Southwest Colorado's oldest existing bank.

When the initial boom of Durango's early years began to slow, the long-distance owners of First National decided to sell to the Bank of Durango. The two banks became the First National Bank of Durango in 1885. Having survived the major fire of 1889, First National Bank of Durango burned down in 1892, and the current building was constructed.

The bank existed here until it moved across the railroad tracks to its present location in 1980-81, almost 100 years after its inception. It is the oldest existing bank in Southwest Colorado.

A LYNCHING

Down 9th Street toward the railroad tracks, Durango's only recorded lynching occurred in 1881, reflecting the general lawlessness of a young town in the throes of growing pains.

On a Sunday morning in a dance hall called The Coliseum, stagecoach driver Henry Moorman killed a local miner, James Prindle, in cold blood. Through the day, an angry crowd formed and grew. Calling themselves a "Committee of Safety," the mob took the law into their hands, dragged Moorman to a pine tree, and hanged him.

Caroline Romney, publisher of the town's first newspaper, the *Durango Record*, described the hanged man: "The pale moonlight glimmering through the rifted clouds clothed the ghastly face with a ghastlier pallor." As for the mob, she wrote, "The Powers that be . . . have proclaimed to the world that good order, peace, quietude, and safety to person and property must and shall prevail in Durango." In fact, it wasn't long before the townspeople created a local government that adopted ordinances to curb unruly behavior.

Look across the street and try to find this interesting leaf motif.

THE ARCHITECTURE

Like a fortress, this building has stood at the northeast corner of 9th and Main since 1892. Its imposing style is known as Richardson Romanesque after Henry Hobson Richardson, a 19th century American architect. Traits of Richardson buildings in this structure include massive stone construction, broad arches, squat columns defining the entrance, and deeply set windows and doors. It was a popular style reflecting prosperous times in the early 1890s.

THREE BANKS

This solid structure first housed the Colorado State Bank, which failed in December 1907. In 1910, Burns National Bank took its place. Named for its founder, **Thomas D. (T.D.) Burns**, the bank was eventually purchased by the Bank of Colorado, which moved in 1995. It has been a restaurant since then.

 You are looking at the **Burns Bank building** – yet another former bank.

THOMAS D. BURNS

T.D. Burns was an Irish immigrant who came to the United States as a child. As a young man in the early 1860s, he drifted west and after unsuccessful endeavors in Colorado, settled in northern New Mexico.

He married a young woman from a wealthy Hispanic family and established several mercantiles, or general stores. Soon, often by dubious means, his wealth and influence increased. He became the first non-Hispanic to acquire interests in the Tierra Amarilla Land Grant, vast properties the Spanish and Mexican governments had granted to settlers long before those territories were annexed by the United States in the Mexican-American War of 1846-48.

As his holdings grew, Burns's affluence and political power increased. He served in the New Mexico territorial legislature and speculated in real estate, sheep, timber, and mining. Opening his own bank in Durango expanded his prosperity and influence. Burns also owned the popular Trimble Hot Springs resort and hotel north of Durango. The hot springs still operates today, though the hotel no longer exists.

SALOON BLOCK

As you walk north, you will pass several buildings that once housed saloons and gambling halls. There were ten in this block, all on this side of Main Avenue, making it the "rough" side of the street, where only men would walk. Ladies stayed on the other side of Main Avenue.

MARSHAL VS. SHERIFF

The town's atmosphere in the early 20th century was, if not lawless, often rowdy and undisciplined. In January 1906, **Sheriff William J. Thompson**, a large man with an intimidating demeanor, quarreled with Marshal Jesse Stansel about who should control gambling in Durango. The two got into a fierce argument in front of the El Moro Saloon at 981 Main Ave., where Thompson had a desk. The sheriff pulled his gun and shot Stansel at close range. Marshal Stansel fired back, hitting Thompson. The sheriff died on the way to the hospital.

Stansel recovered and at trial pleaded self-defense. He was found not guilty. In 1907 he moved to El Paso, Texas, where he continued in law enforcement.

BESSIE RIVERS

At the turn of the century, a legendary madam named Bessie Rivers operated out of the popular Horseshoe Club on this block. The Horseshoe benefited from Bessie's flair for refinement and good taste. Her plush private suite was located on the floor above.

Despite her profession, Bessie was reputed to be an honest and decent citizen. She was deemed charitable, sympathetic, and a shrewd businesswoman. Rivers was the second woman to be allowed to open an account at the First National Bank of Durango, after Estelle Camp, wife of the bank president, A.P. Camp. Bessie retired in 1925 and died in 1937.

14

Stop at the corner of 10th Street and Main Avenue.
Try to find this mural.

You found the mural painted on the north side of the building known as the **Central Hotel**.

THE CENTRAL HOTEL

The building on which the mural is painted was built in 1892 and has most often housed a hotel and/or saloon, but also the La Plata County Bank and a post office. The roof style (called a mansard roof) and the dormer windows on the top floor were inspired by fashionable French architecture and considered sophisticated during the prosperous era of the early 1890s.

In 2006, a fire set by a fourth floor resident of the hotel seriously damaged the upper stories, but the structure has been restored.

DEMPSEY/MALLOY MATCH

The mural pictured on the previous page recalls a 1915 boxing match between Jack Dempsey (fighting under the name "Kid Blackie") and Andy Malloy. The fight actually took place in the **Gem Theatre** across 10th Street in the Jarvis Building. You can read about the fight under the painting.

Although there is some dispute whether Dempsey knocked out Malloy, Dempsey did go on to become the world heavyweight champion four years later. His hometown, Manassa, is in south central Colorado, about 100 miles east of Durango.

Across Main Avenue from the Central Hotel,
try to find this.

 You are looking at the **Schneider building**.

THE BUILDING

The name and date on the pediment tell us R.C. Schneider erected this building in 1889. Originally a men's clothing store, by 1900 the corner property had become the **Palace Grocery and Meat Market**, owned by a man with a similar name, Charles H. Snyder. The business changed hands twice, but remained a grocery store into the late 1940s.

UPSTAIRS

The Keeley Institute, a society to eliminate liquor, opium, and tobacco use, leased offices on the second level of the building. Later, the upper floor was turned into a dance hall that existed into the 1920s.

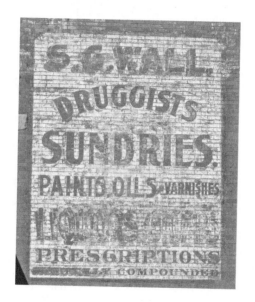

Cross Main Avenue toward the Schneider Building.
Try to find this sign across 10th Street.

S.G. WALL DRUGGIST

In the late 1890s, Sam G. Wall bought a drug store on this site from the original owners, Charles Newman (who built the Newman Building) and his partners, Tom Chestnut and William Stephens. Sam Wall died in 1931, but the building remained a drug store until 1981, when it became a restaurant. Many of the

 You are looking at a building used as a drug store from the 1890s until 1981.

items from the old drug store are on display inside.

Sam Wall's drug store in Durango has no connection to the well-known Wall Drug Store in Wall, South Dakota, which was opened in 1931 by a man named Ted Husted.

LESSONS LEARNED

The northwest corner of the intersection, where the **Jarvis Building** now stands, is where Durango's first major fire broke out on July 1, 1889. Seven blocks of mostly wood businesses, homes, and churches were destroyed. From then on, the city required new construction to be mainly of brick and stone. The Jarvis Building was one such brick structure from the early 1890s, though its appearance has changed over the years. In the early days it had a Victorian era design and was occupied by a candy store, a cobbler, a printer, and a tailor's shop. In 1915, part of the building was turned into a movie house, the Gem Theatre, where the Dempsey-Malloy boxing match took place.

Next to the Jarvis Building is the **Kern Building**. Its upper story façade resembles carved wood, but is made of pressed metal shipped by train from the Mesker Company in St. Louis. Prefabricated metal façades were strong, relatively inexpensive, and fire resistant, making them a popular alternative to wood. The property was owned for many years by the Kern family and housed the Balthasar Kern Saloon, named for the owner, Balthasar "Balsey" Kern.

17

Continue north on Main Avenue to the end of the block and look for
the beautiful dentil work on this hard-to-miss building.

 The architectural details you found are on the **Old Main Post Office**.

DURANGO POST OFFICE

The plaque by the north door tells us this building was built in 1929, and for five decades it housed Durango's main post office. The structure's rectangular shape and the many-paned windows are common to Georgian style architecture, named for the four King Georges of England and popular in Colonial America. The decorative band that resembles teeth below the parapet in the photo is called dentil work. The motif is repeated above the words "U.S. Post Office" over the doors.

GRAND CENTRAL HOTEL

About fifty years before the post office was built, the fashionable Grand Central Hotel was on this corner. It was built by **Thomas Rockwood**, who had run hotels in Silverton, including the Grand Imperial, before coming to Durango. It opened in the fall of 1880, using a small sheet-iron stove to heat the parlor and candles and coal oil lamps for light.

The hotel burned down in the 1889 fire. The last man out of the burning building took a moment to save the hotel register, in which the names of many prominent Durangoans were recorded from the town's earliest days.

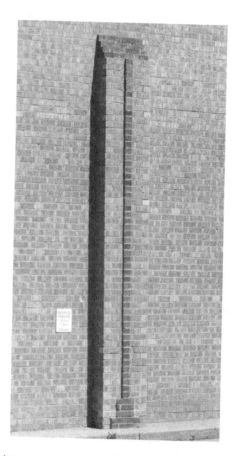

Cross 11th Street and continue north on Main Avenue. Notice this detail on the first building you see.

18

You have found the old Safeway grocery store.

....

SAFEWAY

Post-World War II prosperity brought Durango its first national chain store and self-service grocery shopping in the late 1940s. Up to then, people handed their shopping lists to clerks who pulled items from shelves behind their counters and packaged everything for them. At the Safeway store, shoppers could wander through aisles and take things from the shelves themselves, then pay a clerk, who tallied up what they owed.

DURANGO NEWSPAPERS

Durango's first newspaper was published out of a tent, and subsequent ones have had offices throughout the downtown district.

Arthur and Morley Ballantine bought and merged two newspapers in 1952, eventually renaming the combined paper *The Durango Herald* in 1960. The Ballantines first set up shop next to the Safeway store, in the *Herald Democrat* offices at 1130 Main Ave. After occupying another Main Avenue location for several years, they built the newpaper's current headquarters at 1275 Main Ave. in 1966.

David Day originated the *Herald Democrat* after publishing *The Solid Muldoon* in Ouray. The feisty newspaperman had earned the Medal of Honor after joining the Union Army as a teenager. He named his Ouray paper in honor of wrestling champion William Muldoon, who was known as "The Solid Man."

Day moved to Durango in 1892 and published the *Herald Democrat* until his death in 1914, fearlessly criticizing officials and business owners alike in often colorful language. His son Rod took over, and developed an intense rivalry with William Wood, the editor of a competing newspaper. In 1922, the two brawled about Prohibition. Wood broke Day's nose, at which point Day shot and killed him. Day was acquitted and continued to edit the *Herald Democrat* until 1928, when it was sold.

 Proceed to the corner of 12th and Main and look to the west.

MOUNTAINS AND MINING CAMPS

The mountain behind **Hogsback Ridge** is Perins Peak, named for Charles Perin, a civil engineer who surveyed the original Durango town site in 1880. Beyond the peak, a busy coal mining camp called **Perin** operated in the early 1900s and for a while produced the most coal in the area. The mine closed in 1926.

WALKING DURANGO

19

Turn to your right and walk up 12th Street.
After one block, find this.

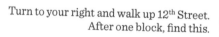

DURANGO HIGH SCHOOL

As you can see from the words on the façade, this was once Durango High School. The school was built in 1916 and served as the local high school for sixty years. Today it houses the Durango School District administration. The original gymnasium is located on the lower level and there was once a swimming pool in the base-

 You have found what was once Durango High School.

ment. Old sports trophies and yearbooks are displayed on the main floor. The building is open to the public on weekdays.

DURANGO PUBLIC LIBRARY ★

On the southeast corner you will see the original **Durango Public Library**, now called the Carnegie Building. It was built in 1907 with a $12,500 grant from steel magnate Andrew Carnegie, one of more than 2,500 libraries around the world funded by the Carnegie Library Foundation.

General William Palmer donated the land for the library and the Ladies Library Association of Durango collected books to fill it. **Sadie Sullivan** was the librarian for 45 years, expanding the book collection from 5,000 to 30,000 volumes. Children especially loved the display of her extensive doll collection. As the library grew, several additions and changes were made to the building. In 2008, the library moved to 1900 E. 3rd Ave. This building now houses city offices.

Continue east on 12th Street another block,
then turn left on 3rd Avenue.
Looking up as you walk along, try to spot this ornate downspout.

The downspout you spotted is on the Hood Mortuary Building, aka the **Amy Mansion**.

AMY MANSION

Hood Mortuary was built in 1888 by Ernest Amy, who was manager of the San Juan & New York Mining and Smelting Company, then the largest business in Durango.

Amy's wife reportedly did not want to come west, so he and her father (one of the smelter owners) had this shingle-style mansion built to lure her here. Resembling popular seaside resort mansions in the northeast, the house was heated and wired for electricity, and the interior was elegantly designed and furnished. It cost $50,000 to build, at least twenty times what the average Durango home cost in the 1880s.

Isabelle Amy did move to Durango and lived here for several years. She and her husband entertained lavishly in their home until 1895 when the San Juan Smelter was sold and the Amys returned east.

HOOD MORTUARY

The Amy mansion remained a private home until 1932, when "Speed" Doran purchased it. Andrew Fuller Hood had established a mortuary on 9th Street in 1902. After his death, his widow sold the business to Doran, who moved it to the former Amy mansion. Thus the house became the Hood Mortuary, retaining that name through subsequent owners. Andrew Hood had owned five mortuaries in the area and at one time served as mayor of Durango.

SMELTING

Durango had two smelters along the Animas River, near the present-day intersection of Highways 160 and 550. They were the only facilities in the area where gold silver, copper, lead—and later uranium—were extracted from ore mined in the region. Smelting heavily contributed to the town's economy, and also filled the air with smoke and the sound of constant noise.

Cross 13th Street and find these distinctive parapets and niches.

EMORY E. SMILEY

Smiley was principal of Durango High School for three years before being promoted to superintendent in 1906. He oversaw construction of the new high school on 12th Street in 1916-17. In 1935, despite the Great Depression, Smiley persuaded Durangoans to pass a $97,000 bond issue and obtained an $86,000 Public Works Administration grant for the junior high school that bears his name.

Emory Smiley was hardworking, modest, and respected. Hoyt Miller, a principal of Smiley Junior High, wrote that Smiley was busy at his desk by 7 a.m. every day and "at 4 p.m. he peremptorily bangs shut his office door and retires to his home. Here he meticulously tends his own lawn with a precision that keeps each blade of grass and every shrub in a state of startled alertness."

Smiley retired in 1943 and died eighteen years later at the age of 88.

 You are looking at the **Smiley Junior High School Building**.

SMILEY JUNIOR HIGH SCHOOL

The Smiley Building was formerly a junior high school, built in 1937. It was Durango's largest federally funded project during the Great Depression, and the city's only junior high school for twenty-three years. It was named for former Durango School District Superintendent Emory E. Smiley.

Constructed in Mission Revival style, the building's arches, parapets, and niches reflect the designs of the 18th and 19th century Spanish missions in California.

The Durango School District decided it no longer needed an educational facility at this site and declared it surplus property in 1995. Private individuals purchased the building in 1997 and transformed the deteriorating school into an energy efficient structure that now houses offices, classrooms, and studios.

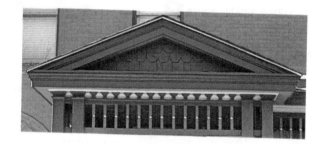

Backtrack across 13th Street and continue south until you find this colorful porch adornment. Along 3rd Avenue, you will find street names in the sidewalk at each intersection.

 The **Wilson/Perkins House** is a fine example of Queen Anne style.

QUEEN ANNE STYLE

The architecture of this well-preserved house is called Queen Anne, a fanciful and elaborate style popular in the 1890s. Notice how the ornate front porch, brightly painted wood trim, and arched window with decorative glass contrast with the natural colors and more rustic informality of the Amy mansion next door.

THE OWNERS

Adair and Margaret Wilson had this house built in 1892. Wilson was an attorney, a state senator, and a judge. Other prominent politicians and businessmen have lived here, including pioneer Durango businessman Robert E. Sloan. **Clayton Perkins** purchased the residence in 1905. Perkins was an early Durango mayor and was married to Zaidee Rockwood, daughter of Thomas Rockwood, who built the Grand Central Hotel on Main Avenue. For a time, the Rockwood family lived next door in the Amy mansion, where the Perkins-Rockwood wedding reception was held in 1901.

Next door you will find this house, built by a successful cattleman.

SENATOR GEORGE WEST

The original inhabitant of this house (until 1912) was State Senator George West. His nickname was "Smoothie." West came to Colorado at the age of 25 with no family and little money. Through hard work and shrewd investment, he became a well-to-do cattleman in the Mancos Valley west of Durango. He served twice as state senator, retired from the cattle business, and became a prominent Durango citizen. West died in 1951 at the age of 99, outliving a wife and two sons.

THE STYLE

The **West House** is a mixture of four major architectural styles. The painted green wood rectangles are early English Tudor; the red tile roof is Spanish; the boxy shape is American Foursquare; and the curved brackets and corbels at roof corners are American Craftsman.

23

Cross 12th Street and look for this.

 The stained glass window you found dates back to 1890.

FIRST PRESBYTERIAN

The **First Presbyterian Church** of Durango, a wood-frame structure, was built on this site in 1882. Destroyed in the 1889 fire, it was rebuilt in 1890. (Note the date on the cornerstone.) The style is Romanesque Revival, based on the architecture of ancient Rome. The arched windows, stone construction, wood-shingled trim, and projecting bell tower are all examples of this style. The stained-glass windows are original, from 1890.

PASTOR McFARLAND

James M. McFarland, the first pastor of the Presbyterian Church, was once kidnapped by a masked man in the middle of the night and forced at gunpoint to a "lonely spot" on the Animas River. More armed men joined them, and McFarland was rudely escorted to the home of a young lady whom the masked stranger intended to marry. The girl's family and friends opposed the marriage but stood by helplessly as the ceremony was performed.

The vows made, the bride and groom and their cohorts fled with the minister at a run. Though McFarland had not yet been ordained, to his knowledge the legality of the marriage was never questioned.

FIRST CHURCH OF CHRIST, SCIENTIST

Across 3rd Avenue is another church, built in the early 1920s in Classical Revival style with symmetrical, balanced proportions and an oculus (eye-like) window. The old high school on 12th Street is another Classical Revival building.

As you continue down 3rd Avenue, look across the street for the house with central double doors.

 You have found the **Bayles/Wigglesworth house**. It is among the oldest buildings in Durango.

A SURVIVOR

This little house, dating from 1882, is distinctive because it survived the 1889 fire and is thus one of the oldest buildings in Durango. A simplified version of Colonial style architecture with its central doors and symmetrical composition, the house has been substantially altered from the original.

THE WIGGLESWORTHS

William Wigglesworth was the best known occupant of the house. William was Durango city manager for many years in the 1920s. He came to Durango in 1881 with his parents, **Thomas and Ann Wigglesworth**.

Nicknamed "Wig," Thomas Wigglesworth surveyed and engineered major portions of the original Durango-area railroad lines, including the Durango to Silverton route for the Denver & Rio Grande and routes to Rico and Farmington, New Mexico, for the Rio Grande Southern Railroad. William followed in his father's footsteps as a railroad surveyor and engineer before working for the city.

Continue south on 3rd Avenue
and look for this porch column detail.

 This unassuming house has many gables, along with a stamped metal roof.

ITALIANATE STYLE

The original portion of this house is a modest version of Italianate architecture, reminiscent of the villas of the Italian Renaissance period. Characteristics of the style are the multi-gabled roof and the slender columns and brackets on the front porch.

BARRIES and SLOANS

James Barrie, a saloon owner, originally owned this house, built in 1885. In 1886, Barrie and his wife divorced, and the property transferred to their daughters.

In 1906, **Robert H. Sloan** and his wife Ada acquired the house and lived here for more than forty years. Robert worked for the Graden Mercantile Company on Main Avenue, founded in the 1880s by his father, Robert E. Sloan, and T.C. Graden. When his father died in 1932, Robert H. took over the presidency of the business.

When Graden mercantile caught fire in 1948, Robert H. was ill at home, and his family was afraid to tell him the news. Finally, his nephew went to his house to give him the report. His reply: "Let 'er burn." He seemed tired of running the business and died shortly thereafter, having served fifty-five years with the Graden firm. After his death, Sloan descendants rebuilt the Graden Mercantile Building.

26

Continue south on 3rd Avenue.
As you approach the corner at 10th Street,
look for this between the sidewalk and the street.

You located an upping stone, adjacent to the **Haggart House.**

UPPING STONES

Before automobiles, structures such as these, called carriage blocks or upping stones, were installed to help riders or passengers mount or dismount a horse or carriage. The blocks might be decorated or not; this one is engraved with the name of the owner of the adjacent house.

HAGGART HOUSE

The house on this corner is another Queen Anne style home, built around 1881. It is one of the oldest brick homes in Durango and survived the 1889 fire. The home is noted for its most prominent resident, Dr. John Haggart, who became the first medical staff president at Mercy Hospital in 1896.

Dr. Haggart performed the first surgery, an appendectomy, in the hospital in July 1897. Mrs. Haggart was among Durango's first residents, arriving as a teenager with her family in January 1881. She attended the University of Denver for two years, then returned to Durango. She was known as a talented performer in Durango Amateur Club entertainments.

UNA PEARSON PROPERTY

Across the boulevard from the Haggart House, an ornamental fence marks the property originally belonging to the John "Jack" Pearson family. On January 31, 1881, his daughter, Una C. Pearson, was the first white child born in Durango. In honor of her birth, a local business gave her parents this plot of land. Jack Pearson, an English-born cattle rancher, built a home and moved his family here when Una was about 5 years old. Recent owners have extensively remodeled the house.

Cross 10th Street and try to spot these unusual eaves.

This roof tops an American Foursquare house.

FOURSQUARE HOUSE

The simple box shape of this house, built partially of local sandstone, is called Foursquare, a style that was popular from the 1890s through the 1930s. Like many Foursquare houses, this one has Craftsman elements including the exposed roof rafters. Inside, these houses typically have four boxy rooms on each floor. In later years, the design was especially popular as mail order houses from such companies as Sears Roebuck. Sloan family descendants have continuously owned the house and keep it as original as possible, both inside and out.

SLOAN FAMILY

Robert E. Sloan, who built this home in 1912, was a cavalry soldier with Gen. William Palmer in the Civil War. After the war, he came to Durango at General Palmer's invitation to work on the Denver & Rio Grande Railway. In the early 1880s he became a partner in the Graden Mercantile Company. When this house was built, the Sloans' adult son, Robert H., lived down the street at 1131 3rd Ave.

Robert E. and Hannah Sloan had another son, Robert S. Sloan, and three daughters, Anne, Jean, and Mary. Through the lineage of Mary Sloan Ayers, Graden Mercantile has remained in the Sloan family for almost 100 years.

Walking along 3rd Avenue, in the middle of the block look up and to your right for this small window.

GOODMAN HOUSE

If you weren't already familiar with Queen Anne architecture, you are likely beginning to recognize some features of these asymmetrical houses. These can include a steep roof with front-facing gable, a porch across the front of the house, decorative columns, and ornamental trim.

 You have found what is called an eyebrow dormer on the **Goodman house**.

EYEBROW DORMERS

The detail in the photo is called an eyebrow dormer, sitting as it does like an eyebrow above the front porch. It is an additional feature typical of Queen Anne homes.

THE GOODMANS

This house has had numerous residents, including Ray Goodman, his wife Edna, and their family. Mr. Goodman was a funeral director in Durango and later took over the **Goodman Paint and Glass store** from his father.

Another person who lived here for a time was Hoyt Miller, a teacher who served as principal of Smiley Junior High School for seventeen years until his death in 1959. Miller Junior High School (now Miller Middle School) was named after him.

Stop at the corner of 3rd Avenue and 9th Street
and find this window.

THE CHURCH

Many churches were built on East 3rd Avenue because the Durango Trust, the railroad's real estate company set up to sell lots in town, gave churches free lots on the boulevard. This building, St. Mark's Episcopal Church, was completed in 1892 to replace a frame building in another location that burned in the 1889 fire.

 You have found St. Mark's Episcopal Church.

Most of the stained glass windows are more than 100 years old. Each of the large leaded glass panels at the bottom of the windows weighs 300 pounds.

THE PARSON

St. Mark's is the oldest organized church in Durango, dating from 1880. The church's first parson, C.M. Hogue, was a popular preacher who is said to have held services in local saloons and gambling halls wearing his cassock and a set of six-shooters. After giving a sermon, he asked the gamblers to make contributions toward building his church.

THE ARCHITECTURE

While most other churches on 3rd Avenue are Classical (Greek or Roman) style, St. Mark's Church is Gothic Revival. This does not mean it derived from the Germanic Goth tribes of the Middle Ages; rather, *gothic* was at one time a derogatory description of any architecture that was not classical. Nevertheless, it is a powerful style often used for churches because of the emotional appeal of its pointed arches, towers, and spires. Famous Gothic churches include Notre Dame Cathedral in Paris and Westminster Abbey in London. The recently constructed **Columbarium gateway** was built to harmonize with the original architecture.

☞ Now turn around and find these two houses.

THE HOUSES

The two Italianate style houses pictured here were built in 1881. Note their similarities, including the bay windows and verandas with Tuscan columns.

NEWMAN, STEPHENS, and THE CHESTNUTS

The original owners of these houses, Charles Newman (929 E. 3rd Ave.) and William L. Stephens (909 E. 3rd Ave.), were married to sisters, Marian Chestnut Newman and Mary Chestnut Stephens. Tom Chestnut, the brother of Marian and Mary, was a business partner of Newman and Stephens. The three partners owned drug stores at various times in Del Norte, Alamosa, and Silverton, and in Durango at 10th Street and Main Avenue (later sold to S.G. Wall).

Charles Newman was a prominent Durango citizen who built the Newman Building on Main Avenue and was elected to the Colorado Senate in the 1890s.

Cross 9th Street and continue south on 3rd Avenue, noticing this little house along the way.

GOVERNMENT HOUSING

In contrast to many of the stately older homes on 3rd Avenue, this prefabricated one-story frame house dates from the World War II era when large numbers of returning veterans required dwellings for themselves and their families.

The ensuing housing shortage caused "government modular" houses like these to become common in the 1940s because they were inexpensive and easy to assemble. This particular house was moved here from Whiterock, New Mexico (near Los Alamos).

Cross 8th Street and continue south on 3rd Avenue, looking for this post between the sidewalk and the street.

Imagine horses tied up in front of these homes rather than automobiles lining the street.

THE CAMP FAMILY HOME

Note the interesting detailing around the windows and door of the house and at the peaks of the roof. This decorative detailing is called Stick style because it is flat against the house (not three-dimensional) with emphasis on pattern and line. The colors of the house today are the same as they were in the 1880s.

THE CAMP FAMILY

The original owner of this handsome residence was one of Durango's most influential citizens, A.P. Camp, of the First National Bank of Durango. He and his wife Estelle were active in the business, political, cultural, and social lives of Durango for many years, from the mid-1880s to well past the turn of the century. **Estelle Camp** had attended Cornell University before her marriage. As a civic leader in Durango, she campaigned for planting of trees on 3rd Avenue, construction of the library, and creation of Mesa Verde National Park.

The Camps' only surviving son, Alfred McNeil Camp, attended the University of Virginia. He became vice-president of First National Bank of Durango under his uncle, John McNeil, when his father died in 1925. Four years later, he was named president and remained so for twenty-five years. Except for his college years, he lived in this house his entire life, from 1884 until his death in 1970.

From the Camp house, retrace your steps to 8th Street and turn left toward 2nd Avenue. Before turning left again at 2nd, look to your right to find these blue panels.

WEST BUILDING

Midway down the block on the west side of 2nd Avenue, this four-story office structure stands out from surrounding buildings.

In the 1950s, when gas and oil were discovered in the region, Durango wanted to attract highly paid corporate executives, engineers, and geologists. Developers James and Ward West erected this building to provide offices for them. They chose the sleek, big city International style, using glass, steel, and con-

You have found the **West Building**, a modern International style structure.

crete, which was very popular for commercial buildings throughout the country at the time. The style evolved from the designs of such European architects as Le Corbusier, Ludwig Mies van der Rohe, and Walter Gropius, who developed their techniques in the 1920s.

The design included plans for another four floors, which were never built. At its peak, five oil and gas companies had headquarters in the building, while oilfield service companies and operations centers were located in Farmington, New Mexico. Natural gas development remains a linchpin of La Plata County's economy.

DURANGO ARTS CENTER

On the northeast corner of 2nd Avenue and 8th Street is the Durango Arts Center, a focal point for art and cultural activities. It is housed in a 1920s-era building that was once a car dealership and an auto repair shop. For many years before and after World War II, numerous auto-related business were located on Main and 2nd Avenues.

Now turn left and continue south on 2nd Avenue until you see this.

 The **Rochester Hotel** is a simple building built in the 1890s.

THE ROCHESTER HOTEL

Unlike most of the fashionable, traditional, and classical homes and churches on 3rd Avenue, the Rochester Hotel was built in a local adaptation of the popular Italianate style commercial buildings, featuring tall, hooded rectangular windows and decorative brick cornice. Porches and balconies have been added and altered over the years to embellish the façade.

Originally known as the Peeples Hotel, the structure was built by E.T. Peeples in 1891. It has had numerous owners, including Mary Francis Finn (1905-1920), who changed the name to the Rochester for unknown reasons. Over the years, the hotel's success followed the economic ups and downs of the town, at times a popular short-term accommodation for salesmen and tourists, at others a boarding house for less well-to-do clients.

The current owners bought the property in 1992 and completely refurbished the 100-year-old building after it had fallen into disrepair. The décor of the renovated hotel is inspired by the many Western movies filmed in and around Durango, including *She Wore a Yellow Ribbon* and *The Searchers* with John Wayne, *How the West Was Won* and *Cheyenne Autumn* with Jimmy Stewart, and in the 1980s and '90s, *National Lampoon's Vacation* and *City Slickers*.

LELAND HOUSE

Across the street from the Rochester Hotel stands the **Leland House**, built by Durango builder P.W. Pittman in 1927. In the 1930s he managed the Pittman Motor Company, a Ford dealership in the 900 block of Main Avenue. He lived in a house at 10th Street and 3rd Avenue that had originally belonged to the Una Pearson family. First called Pittman Apartments, Leland House, named for subsequent owner Leland Hill, became a bed and breakfast in 1993.

Continue south to 7th Street and turn left to return to 3rd Avenue. Crossing 7th Street, be on the lookout for this porch across the boulevard.

 You have found the **Weightman House**.

....

WEIGHTMAN HOUSE

In the 1890s Walter Weightman built this large, attractive home for his family. The lacy ornamental details of the house, especially the porch spindles with their fancy buttons and knobs, are called Eastlake style after Charles Eastlake, a late 19th century English furniture designer. The spacious main floor of the home was the site of many church socials, receptions, and teas through the years the Weightman family lived here.

WALTER WEIGHTMAN and MUNROE FIELDS

Walter Weightman was born in England and came to the western United States in 1879. He opened a grocery store with two partners in Animas City. The grocery was moved to Durango in 1881 where Mr. Weightman prospered, soon investing with T.C. Graden and Robert Sloan in the Graden Mercantile Company. His grocery was one of the largest and finest in the state.

The second owner of the house, Munroe Fields, was a well-to-do Durango businessman and rancher. He was at one time vice-president of the Burns Bank on Main Avenue. He bought the house in 1917 but was unable to move his family in due to the flu epidemic of 1918. He had to find a temporary dwelling for his wife and five children until they recovered from the flu in order to avoid a quarantine on the house.

34

Continue south on 3rd Avenue.
Try to find these rough-hewn stone blocks on your right.

➤➤ The stones you found were all cut by hand.

....

DUTCH COLONIAL 🏠

David Ramsey, a Scottish stone-mason, built this Dutch Colonial Revival style house in 1906. He shaped the stone blocks using a mallet and chisel. The most notable characteristic of the house is its barn-like shape. The roof is called a gambrel roof because it resembles the hip of a horse's hind leg, the "gambrel" joint. Often, this style house is turned sideways so that the front door is on the long side of the house and the peaked gables are on the ends.

THE MACLEANS

A later owner of the house, Maggie Jane MacLean, was also from Scotland. Her brother Daniel, who lived here with his sister for a time in the 1920s, was involved in mining and smelting in the Durango area around the turn of the 20th century. He owned the Highland Mary Mine near Silverton.

35

Continue south on 3rd Avenue
and look for a house with an unusually steep roof.

 You have found the **Keegan House.**

THE KEEGAN HOUSE

An Irish railroad contractor named Peter Keegan built this house in Queen Anne style in 1881. In the early 1900s, another owner added the steep roof and tower-shaped dormer. The St. Columba Catholic church congregation used the house until their church was completed in 1881.

A WESTERN GUN BATTLE

Indicative of the unruliness of the early Durango years, Peter Keegan's family was once trapped in the crossfire of a gun battle on this site. A group of cowboys from nearby Farmington, New Mexico, caught the lawless Stockton-Eskridge gang, of the Durango area, stealing their cattle. Keegan's family, who were living at the time in a large tent on the property while their house was being built, had the misfortune of being in the path of the resulting skirmish. They were forced to take cover under a feather bed until Keegan arrived to talk the cowboys into letting them escape.

At this point, the tour of 3rd Avenue concludes. Crossing College Drive at the light on your return to Main Avenue, you will be standing on the corner where the Cliff Brice Service Station once stood. It opened in 1941, facing what was then 6th Street, and remained in business for about 50 years. In those days, station attendants filled your gas tank, cleaned your windshield, and checked your oil before taking your cash and bringing you change. At its peak, the Pueblo-based company had 75 Cliff Brice Stations throughout the Rocky Mountain states. After the service station closed, the building remained for several years before it was demolished and replaced by the current structures.

Continue west on College toward Main. The south side of the street on your left has gradually transformed from a residential area to a more business-oriented stretch. The early homes here belonged principally to ethnic working-class citizens, many of them Hispanic.

Approaching Main Avenue, look to your right. The Sixth Street Station on the northeast corner of College and Main was another of several service stations in this part of town until late in the twentieth century.

Great Finish!

You are now close to where the tour began. We hope it has led you to see Durango in a new light. Maybe you'll envision Utes encamped on Main Avenue or imagine the Stockton-Eskridge gang disrupting the peaceful homes on 3rd Avenue. Perhaps building styles will stand out for you, or you'll wonder what it was like to swim in the old high school's basement pool.

If you've enjoyed learning about Durango's history and want to know more, we have lots of places you can find stories and photos from our past:

> Animas Museum, 3065 West 2nd Avenue
> Durango Discovery Museum, 1333 Camino del Rio
> Durango Public Library, 1900 East 3rd Avenue
> Durango & Silverton Narrow Gauge Railroad Museum,
>   479 Main Avenue
> Fort Lewis College Center of Southwest Studies, 1000 Rim Drive
> Southern Ute Cultural Center and Museum,
>   356 Ouray Drive in Ignacio

To learn about other things to see and do in Durango, visit:
> Durango Arts Center, 802 East 2nd Avenue
> Durango Area Tourism Office, 111 South Camino del Rio
> Durango Welcome Center, 802 Main Avenue
> San Juan Public Lands Center, 15 Burnett Court

TO LEARN MORE

Aleo, Philip A. *The Strater Hotel Story*. Dundee, Ill.: Aleo Publications, 2009.

* La Plata County Historical Society, *Historic Durango*, Vols. IX-XVIII. Durango, various.

* La Plata County Historical Society records: Colorado Cultural Resource Surveys.

* Sarah Platt Decker Chapter, D.A.R. *Pioneers of the San Juan Country, Vol. IIV*. Colorado Springs, Colo., 1942-1961

Smith, Duane A. *Durango Diary*. Durango, CO: The Herald Press, 1996.

—- *Durango Diary II 1890s-1945*. Durango, CO: Durango Herald Small Press, 2007.

—- *Guide to Durango & Silverton*. Evergreen, CO: Cordillera Press, 1991.

—- *Rocky Mountain Boom Town: A History of Durango, Colorado*. Niwot, CO: University Press of Colorado, 1980, 1986, 1992.

Wildfang, Frederic B. *Hollywood of the Rockies*. Durango: The Rochester Hotel, 1997

—- *Images of America, Durango*. Charleston, S. C.: Arcadia Publishing, 2009.

* available at the Animas Museum

ACKNOWLEDGMENTS

A sincere thank you to the following individuals for their inspiration, guidance, assistance, and encouragement in the creation of this book: Ann Butler, *The Durango Herald*; Robert McDaniel, Brianna McCormick, and the Animas Museum staff; Duane Smith, Fort Lewis College; Elizabeth Green, Lisa Atchison, Robert and Nancy Whitson, and Jennifer O'Donohue, Durango Herald Small Press; Diane Burress, Marty Kay Hutton, and Jane Schold, Durango School District 9-R; Susan Davies, Graden Mercantile Company; Dennis Johnson, Stuart's of Durango; Nik Kendziorski, Center of Southwest Studies, Fort Lewis College; Kirk Komick, Rochester and Leland House Hotels; Kathy McKenzie, La Plata County Historical Society board; Jill Seyfarth, Cultural Resource Planning; Vicki Vandegrift, City of Durango; my wonderful first editor, Jeanne Moody; my friends and writing colleagues, Karin, Kim, Rose, and Wendy; and friends and family who generously lent help and support.

Peggy Winkworth is a writer who has lived in Durango for fifteen years. While vacationing in Key West, she saw a walking tour guide and had an idea: why not develop a similar guide for Durango? It might be a scavenger hunt to appeal to children. Then a college-sponsored guided tour caused her to realize that a fun and informative book about Durango could appeal to all ages.

"Writing the book has taught me a great deal about this town," Peggy says. "I hope readers will enjoy and learn from *Walking Durango: History, Sights, and Stories* as much as I have."

PHOTO CREDITS

Present day color photos by the author.
All historic photos courtesy of La Plata County Historical Society
unless otherwise noted:

P. 8 depot crowd, Center of Southwest Studies (CSWS), Fort Lewis College; p. 12 The Grande Palace, CSWS; p. 22 Henry Strater, Strater Hotel; p. 30 Main Mall fire, *Durango Herald*; p. 34 A.P. Camp, CSWS; p. 36 T.D. Burns, SOS SN7036, Const. Convention book, New Mexico State Records Center & Archives; p. 78 Estelle Camp, CSWS.

INDEX

CPSIA information can be obtained at www.ICGtesting.com
Printed in the USA
LVOW02s1847100913

351829LV00024B/52/P